MORTGAGE LOAN OFFICER SUCCESS GUIDE

MORTGAGE LOAN OFFICER SUCCESS GUIDE

MICHAEL ZUREN, PHD

Copyright © 2016 Michael Zuren, PhD
All rights reserved.

ISBN-13: 9781539089957
ISBN-10: 1539089959
Library of Congress Control Number: 2016916465
CreateSpace Independent Publishing Platform
North Charleston, South Carolina

This book is dedicated to my friend John "Jeff" Paul. He has been an invaluable inspiration and motivation to me, from his selfless actions and dedication to helping others. He has always displayed concern and kindness to his friends, family, and associates. I would like to thank him for his encouragement and for the exemplary values and ethics he has exhibited through his endeavors. He set an example that hard work, sacrifice, achievement, and integrity will overcome the struggles often faced in life.

ACKNOWLEDGMENTS

I would like to thank the loan officers who have mentored me throughout my career, including Thomas Damen and Matthew "Mike" Thomas, who gave their time and shared their personal experiences in the mortgage profession, which gave meaning and purpose to this book. They were both an inspiration and offered great encouragement during my journey in completing this project. Finally, I thank my children, Christopher, Zachary, Delaney, and Gracie, who supported me with their love and understanding of the commitment needed to complete one of my life's ambitions.

CONTENTS

Dedication v
Acknowledgments vii
Preface xiii

Chapter 1 1
  Introduction to Mortgage Banking 1
  Educational Licensing Requirements 4
  Choosing the Right Employer and Environment 5
  Investigate the Company's Reputation 6
  Product Knowledge and Guidelines (Conventional,
    FHA, VA, USDA, 203k) 7
  Conventional Mortgage 8
  FHA Mortgage 8
  VA Mortgage 9
  USDA/RHS Mortgage 9
  Finding Your Niche 10

Chapter 2 12
- Business Plan 12
- Creating Your Living Business Plan 14
- Finding a Mentor 16
- Time Management 17
- Conclusion 18

Chapter 3 19
- Building a Referral Base 19
- Relationship-Building Strategies 20
- How to Build Relationships 23
- Customer-Service Skills 29
- How to Develop Referral Sources 32
- Keeping Your Past Customers for Life 42
- The Importance of Customer Service 46

Chapter 4 50
- Customer Service 50
- Following the Transaction 53
- Keeping All Parties Informed 54
- Benefits of Quality Customer Service 57
- Past-Customer Testimonials and
  Endorsements (Brag Book) 59

Chapter 5 61
- Social Media and Other Lead Sources 61
- Create Your Own Content 64
- Social Media 66
- Position Yourself as an Expert 68

Chapter 6 · 70
  How to Create Your Marketing/Advertising Budget · · · 70
  Marketing Plan · 73
  Business Plan · 74
Chapter 7 · 78
  Networking · 78
  Membership and Group Participation · · · · · · · · · · · 81
Chapter 8 · 85
  Accepting Change and Thriving · · · · · · · · · · · · · · · 85
  Creating a Winning Marketing Plan · · · · · · · · · · · · 86
  Staying Current on Product Guidelines and
      Regulatory Changes · 87
  Conclusion · 88

PREFACE

Whether you are just starting your career or you have twenty years' experience in the mortgage industry, this book will help you find the right company to help enable you to become proficient and focus on the essential activities that will make you successful. During my twenty-seven-year career as a licensed loan officer, I have had the pleasure of being mentored by highly successful loan officers. Through their experiences and mine, this book captures their successes, failures, life-changing events, words of wisdom, and aha moments. Chapter 1 reviews the essentials, which include knowledge, choosing the right employer, and laying the foundation for success. Chapter 2 delves into building your business plans and the essential aspects for long-term profitability. Chapter 2 also discusses how to create your living business plan to stay on track and maintain consistent business. Chapter 3 reviews the foundation for building lasting referral relationships. Chapter 4 reviews the value and importance of exceptional customer service. Chapters 5, 6, and 7 review other lead sources in creating your marketing plan and networking relationships. Chapter 8 then ties everything together, creating a plan of action to become a highly productive mortgage loan officer. The information in the book will help you avoid costly mistakes and shorten the time needed to achieve your financial goals. Planning, determination, hard work, and knowledge are your keys to success.

Chapter 1

INTRODUCTION TO MORTGAGE BANKING

The mortgage banking profession can be extremely lucrative. If you are thinking about becoming a mortgage loan officer or considering entering the mortgage banking profession, you must realize it is not a nine-to-five occupation. It will impact your personal life, family relationships, and private time. Even if you are not available all hours of the day, you will end up taking problems home, thinking about them and about how you can resolve issues. No matter how hard you try, the problems will find you; it is definitely not an easy job. Successful mortgage loan officers typically work very long hours, answer their phone on the weekends, and take their phone and laptop with them when they go on vacation. Their success relies on hard work, dedication, and devotion to their job. Once you are acclimated to this profession, you will understand that the greater the income, the greater the amount of stress you will have to manage. Success comes with lost deals, spinning your wheels on unfavorable transactions, denied loans, and unruly and demanding clients. The key to your success is your ability to provide exceptional customer service, staying knowledgeable regarding changing guidelines and governmental regulations, and maintaining an unfettered focus to achieve your financial goals.

Highly successful loan officers know how to manage their efforts, money, and time to achieve their goals. Most loan officers make phone calls to their clients well past eight o'clock each night. It is not unusual for clients to be qualified at eight in the morning, ten at night, or on a Sunday afternoon. Long, demanding hours and little private time are just part of being a successful loan officer. The more accommodating and flexible you are with your time, the higher your income will be. You must be prepared for overwhelming stress, cutthroat competition, unmanageable deadlines, complaining support staff, and unobtainable opportunities. If you think you can handle the pressure and manage conflicting personalities, the mortgage loan officer occupation may be the most lucrative career you will ever have.

Mortgage loan officers have many responsibilities. They are required to solicit their lead sources (sphere of influence) to find new prospects for residential mortgage loans. They are required to identify, develop, and maintain a network of relationships that give them recurring referrals to prospective homebuyers. Typically, these referral sources would come from real-estate professionals, social media, builders, attorneys, insurance agents, other lenders, and other referral sources from their sphere of influence. When the loan officer receives a prospective client, he or she needs to have the ability to qualify the borrower and analyze his or her employment, income, debts, and credit history to determine if he or she is able to qualify for a mortgage product. If the potential customer does not qualify for a mortgage, the loan officer must counsel the client, giving him or her step-by-step instructions on how to qualify for a mortgage. The counseling could include credit advice, explanation of mortgage guidelines, or possibly how a cosigner may help him or her qualify for a mortgage. Thorough knowledge of the product guidelines and regulatory requirements is required for success as a loan officer. In addition to these competencies, a loan officer must provide exceptional customer service by overseeing the loan process and keeping all parties involved in the transaction informed, from application to closing the loan. This includes collecting any documentation required to complete the mortgage loan as necessitated by loan guidelines, processing, underwriting, or the closing department. Thorough understanding of the complete mortgage process is necessary for a high level of customer satisfaction. While managing ongoing transactions, a successful loan officer must continue prospecting, generating leads, and maintaining a reasonable level of knowledge on mortgage product guidelines and regulatory changes.

EDUCATIONAL LICENSING REQUIREMENTS

There has been a flurry of legislation because of the mortgage meltdown of 2007. The first such act was the Secure and Fair Enforcement Act of 2008, more commonly known as the SAFE Act. This legislation required that all mortgage loan officers become licensed and meet annual continuing-education requirements. The continuing-education requirement consists of a total of eight hours annually. This is broken down into three hours of federal law and regulations, two hours of ethics, two hours of training related to standards, and one hour of undefined instruction on mortgage origination. Initially, mortgage loan officers had to complete twenty-four hours of education and pass a comprehensive national test as well as complete a background check to earn a license to originate mortgages.

Since 2008, there has been a great deal of legislation passed by Congress to oversee mortgage banking, such as the Dodd-Frank Act, and newly created regulatory agencies, such as the Consumer Finance Protection Bureau (CFPB), which monitors and governs all financial institutions. This legislation and the governing agency were created to protect the public from unscrupulous individuals in financial professions. Although the legislation mandates imposed upon financial institutions and mortgage lenders have eliminated most of the unsavory characters in the banking, lending, and investment professions and particularly minimized the amount of fraud that occurs in mortgage originations, it has also been a great hindrance to individuals obtaining mortgage loans. Many individuals, such as the self-employed, have been completely eliminated as potential homeowners, as well as low-income and credit-impaired households. The mortgage industry has been changed drastically over the last eight years because of the massive amount of legislation and regulation imposed on the industry. Successful loan officers will have to carefully weave themselves through regulations, guidelines, and customer expectations. Because of the massive amount of regulatory hurdles and restrictive guidelines, thoroughly explaining the mortgage process to your customers is imperative to your success.

CHOOSING THE RIGHT EMPLOYER AND ENVIRONMENT

The lending institution you work for will have a direct impact on your success and income. It is important to thoroughly check out a lender's reputation, ability to close loans on time, product selection, and pricing. It would also be very helpful to find out how much the top loan officers at the company make, which will tell you what your potential income limitations are.

* Does the company have a good reputation?
* Do they close their loans on time?
* Do they specialize in any specific loan product?
* How long do loan officers stay at the company (turnover rate)?
* What has the most successful loan officers' average income been over the past few years?

INVESTIGATE THE COMPANY'S REPUTATION

Talk to your real-estate, title, and mortgage contacts in the industry. Does the company have a good reputation?

Do they offer good service and close their loans on time?
Is the company consumer friendly?
What products do they offer?
Are their rates competitive?
What are the process, underwriting, and closing systems?

If it is a new company, research the owner and managers' track record to find out their past successes and failures, to estimate the probable stability of the company. Have you worked with some employees of the company in the past? Can you find out how much financial backing the company has? Even though it's a start-up company, they may have substantial assets and may be run by very competent individuals. When making a decision on a new company try to gather as much information as possible before discounting an opportunity.

Does the company cater to your niche? Have you specialized in a specific mortgage program? Does your sphere of influence recognize you as a specialized mortgage lender?

Depending on your specialty or niche, a small mortgage broker or lender may be the best for you and for your business. If you have worked with employees of the company in the past, ask them what they like and dislike about the company:

* Are they happy or complaining?
* Do they like working at the company?
* Is it a pleasant and flexible environment?

* What position are you being offered (loan officer, branch manager, sales manager, or trainer)?
* Is it a good fit for you at this point in your career?
* Is there room for advancement?
* Is the compensation worth the risk?

Before accepting or declining any new position, especially at a small or start-up company, it is advantageous to research and obtain as much information to make a rational decision. Risk, reward, and the value of the experience are all important factors when considering new job opportunities.

PRODUCT KNOWLEDGE AND GUIDELINES (CONVENTIONAL, FHA, VA, USDA, 203K)

A loan officer's success depends mainly on sales ability and knowledge of loan products and guidelines. The greater the knowledge, the better he or she will be able to meet his or her clients' individual needs. There are four main types of mortgage loans. Each of them has different guidelines on employment, credit history, debt ratio, asset requirements, and property standards. Understanding the underwriting differences will help you decide which mortgage type is right for your client.

The four main loan types are as follows: conventional, Federal Housing Administration (FHA), United States Department of Veterans Affairs (VA), and United States Department of Agriculture (USDA-RHS loans). Below is a description of each mortgage type and some of their major differences.

CONVENTIONAL MORTGAGE

Conventional mortgages follow guidelines issued by Fannie Mae and Freddie Mac, which set the maximum mortgage amount, property requirements, credit standards, debt-to-income guidelines, and down-payment minimums. The current single-family conforming mortgage limit is $417,000. Conventional loans can be fixed, variable, or balloon mortgages. This mortgage type is typically packaged with other conventional mortgages and sold as mortgage-backed securities.

FHA MORTGAGE

The United States Department of Housing and Urban Development (HUD) administers FHA loans. FHA loans require a 3.50 percent down payment, which can be a gift from a relative or down-payment assistance from an eligible source. The credit standards for this loan type are the easiest to qualify for. This loan type also has certain guidelines that other loan types do not have that cater to individuals with deferred student loans, past bankruptcies or foreclosures, rental income, and other income sources (child support, alimony, entitlement income). The maximum mortgaged amount is set per state and county. For most areas, FHA loans can be well into the $200,000 range for a single-family dwelling. FHA also offers rehabilitation loans, which allow monies to be added to a mortgage for repairs or improvements. FHA loans charge an up-front mortgage insurance premium on all loans and a monthly mortgage insurance premium up to

0.85 percent annually. The monthly mortgage insurance is charged for the life of the loan.

VA MORTGAGE

The VA loan is guaranteed by the United States Department of Veterans Affairs. This loan type is exclusively for veterans or service personal to obtain loans at competitive rates and terms with no down payment or mortgage insurance. The VA does not lend money directly to the borrower; it only guarantees the lender will recover 25 percent of the mortgaged amount if the veteran goes into default. The maximum mortgaged amount is generally $417,000 in most areas. The underwriting loan standards for this loan type are looser than conventional loans. This loan type accepts lower credit scores, only one debt ratio is considered, and typically no reserves are required of the borrower. To qualify for a VA loan, one must be a veteran, active-duty personnel, reservist, or National Guard member with an honorable discharge. A surviving spouse may also be eligible for this loan type if certain conditions are met.

USDA/RHS MORTGAGE

The US Department of Agriculture guarantees rural housing loans. This loan type requires no down payment but has a monthly maintenance fee similar to private mortgage insurance. This loan type is only available in designated rural areas. Please refer to the USDA website for specific locations. Income qualifications for this loan type allow applicants to earn up to 115 percent of the median household income for the area. In certain circumstances, USDA loans allow buyers' closing costs to be rolled into the loan (up to 3 percent of the sale price). USDA loans have a 1 percent up-front mortgage insurance premium; in addition, they have a monthly insurance premium of 0.35 percent annually. The USDA also has a program whereby very-low-income families can apply for a mortgage directly through a USDA office and qualify for a special interest rate.

Everyone's situation is different. Understanding the basic guidelines of each mortgage type may assist homebuyers in making the best decision when financing their next home.

* How do I set myself apart from the competition?
* What is different about the services or products that I offer?
* What are the "extras" that I bring to the market?

FINDING YOUR NICHE

Being a niche lender will help you become an expert in your market. Real estate agents and your sphere of influence will think of you first when a particular mortgage type is needed. Niche lenders have greater income stability than standard lenders. Below is a list of questions you can ask yourself to find the perfect mortgage niche for you.

* Who could use specific loan products (such as veterans, investors, or first-time homebuyers)?
* Who will benefit the most from my service?
* Before I devote my time and effort to learn the ins and outs of a certain mortgage type, which one do I already know the most about?

Identify your ideal client and describe his or her situation and mortgage needs. Now identify how you can reach your audience. Are there other businesses and organizations you can network with, such as builders, contractors, insurance agents, CPAs, or nonprofit organizations?

Chapter 2

BUSINESS PLAN

A business plan is a plan of action created to ensure all avenues are being employed for success. Many business plans start with the end goal in mind. For instance, your goal may be $200,000 in annual income. When creating your business plan, you must carefully consider your strengths and weaknesses, time, and financial resources you have to achieve your goals. Always set realistic goals. Building upon last year's sales and income, as well as understanding the current market situation, should play an important role in creating your business plan. An example of a basic business plan is as follows:

1. Income Goal for the Calendar Year
   (Last year's income per transaction, average mortgaged amount, and commission rate should all be considered when determining your income goal)

2. Sales Needed to Reach Desired Goal (Lead Sources)
   A. Networking
   B. Mailings per Month
   C. Prospects
   D. Past Customers
   E. Farming Area
3. Contact Potential Alternative Lead Sources
   A. Mortgage Companies, Banks, and Credit Unions
   B. Title Companies
   C. Interoffice Referrals
   D. Builders
4. Update Active Loans Weekly (buyer, seller, selling agent, and listing agent)
5. Attend Sales Meetings, Share Ideas, Listen to Other Successful Loan Officers' Advice
6. Attend Educational and Motivational Seminars
7. Calculate the Amount of Time Needed to Devote to Your Business Per Week
   A. Daily
   B. Deduct for Days Off
   C. Deduct for Vacations

A business plan is a formal statement of goals and how they will be attained.

Business plans may target changes in perception and branding by the customer. An annual business plan should be both internally and externally focused. Externally focused plans typically have detailed tasks, attempting to reach certain goals.

Internally focused business plans target intermediate goals required to reach the external goals. These tasks may cover everything from adding assistants, delegating duties, new product introductions, new services, and new marketing activities.

A solid business plan should answer the following questions:

* What niche will it fill?
* What are the problems it will solve?
* Who are the company's customers, and how will you market the mortgage products to them?
* Who are the competitors, and how will you maintain a competitive advantage?

It is essential for you to research your competitors and how they get their business, their processes, and their strengths and weaknesses.

Marketing and Sales: How will you market and advertise your business?

CREATING YOUR LIVING BUSINESS PLAN

Your business plan is supposed to be a guide and a reference. It's a live document that you can review and add new ideas on a consistent basis. It is your guide to keep you focused, on task, and motivated as you grow your business and profits.

MORTGAGE LOAN OFFICER SUCCESS GUIDE

Let your business plan grow with you as your business and sphere of influence grows.

Production Goal Worksheet

Month	Jan	Feb	Mar	Apr	May	June	July	Aug	Sep	Oct	Nov	Dec
Pre-approvals												
Loan Applications												
Closed Loans												
Average Loan Size												

Set your goals and then track your success. Adjust your marketing efforts accordingly to meet your objectives.

Daily Schedule Template

Task/Day	Monday	Tuesday	Wednesday	Thursday	Friday	Saturday
Phone Calls						
Emails						
Mailings						
Follow-up Pre-Approvals						
Follow-up Listing Agents						
Follow-up Selling Agents						
Follow-up Buyers in Process						

Weekly/Monthly Plan Template

Task/Day	Monday	Tuesday	Wednesday	Thursday	Friday	Saturday
Sales Calls						
Office Presentations						
Seminars						
CE Classes for Real Estate Agents						
Joint Marketing						
Networking						

FINDING A MENTOR

Many successful loan officers learn the ins and outs of mortgage finance from an experienced and highly successful mentor early on in the development of their career. Establishing the mentor relationship will create firsthand knowledge of what it took to become successful. Instantly applying these traits and activities to your business plan will eliminate sales by trial and error and increase the odds of your success. You may assist your mentors with their daily sales functions, such as sales presentations, writing and placing advertisements, and updating real-estate agents on existing transactions. During this process, you will increase your knowledge of the mortgage profession and learn the necessary information to become successful. Guidance and advice from the mentor is an invaluable commodity, resulting in experiences needed in the mortgage profession.

An effective mentor will be able to evaluate the positive traits and characteristics of the mentee and develop a plan that enhances and builds necessary attributes for a successful career in mortgage banking. A good mentor will direct a mentee on the most effective ways to complete certain tasks and develop necessary skills. It is essential for newly licensed loan officers to develop competencies, gain confidence, and hone their abilities quickly, due to the nature of commission-based compensation in mortgage banking. The transfer of knowledge, experience, and confidence from mentor to mentee is essential to the short and long-term success of a newly licensed mortgage loan originator.

TIME MANAGEMENT

Mortgage loan officers are typically commission based; therefore, their time is money. Developing a system that efficiently uses time will not only increase income, but it will relieve other pressures that accompany self-employment. Effective time management will allow you to maximize your time and increase your accomplishments. Planning your day by creating a priority list of tasks to be completed will allow one to focus on these activities. Creating a list of other tasks that need to be completed by a certain date or that could be delegated will allow time to focus on more important activities. Prioritizing tasks creates focus and proficiency.

Tips to develop a plan based on efficiency and time management:

1. Create a to-do list.
2. Prioritize tasks from the most important to the least important.
3. Create set office hours. Start work at 8:00 a.m. to complete the necessary tasks of the day.
4. Immediately respond to phone calls and e-mails that are priorities each day; respond to other less important phone calls and e-mails later in the day, when other necessary tasks have been completed.
5. Use drive time to respond to voicemails and follow up with active prospective buyers.
6. Set aside time each day just for prospecting and promoting your business.

7. Develop a sphere of influence that will be advocates for your business.
8. Qualify and pull credit reports on all prospective buyers. Do not waste your time on the prospects if they are not ready to buy. If someone cannot be qualified, offer him or her direction so that he or she can qualify for a mortgage in the future.
9. Use a mortgage prospecting and contact management system.

CONCLUSION

Utilizing the above worksheets will allow you to develop your own personal business plan. Start by determining your income goal for the year, based off of last year's production. If you are a new loan officer, start with a realistic number such as two closed loans per month and adjust accordingly throughout the year. Next, determine the number of prospects and sales needed to meet your goals. Determine the number of contacts needed weekly to reach your annual goals, and keep track of your activity with the weekly tracking worksheet. Using the daily schedule of activities worksheet will help you focus throughout each day and help you effectively use your time.

Chapter 3

BUILDING A REFERRAL BASE

Build a Referral Base (Past-Customers Database)
Your past customers are the lifeblood of your business. It takes far more time and money to gain a new customer than to maintain a relationship with a past customer. Connecting with a past customer on a regular basis through phone calls, e-mails, and mailings is a great way to maintain a relationship. A follow-up call when the house transfers and a mailing just to say "thank you and congratulations on the purchase of your new home" will likely increase referrals from past clients and will let your customer know you will be around to help him or her after the transaction is completed. Building a file on each customer to keep the line of communication open with your past customers could include birthdays, the anniversary date of the purchase of

the house, the number of houses he or she owns, and his or her occupation. It is important to maintain a regular communication line with your past customers, such as once every four months, possibly via a call to see if they need your expertise or if a new program or a rate update exists for possible refinancing. Create a sense of loyalty with your past customers; it is the fastest and least expensive avenue to referral business.

RELATIONSHIP-BUILDING STRATEGIES

Successful loan officers stress relationship building as a means to long-term success. Relationship building includes developing an open communication system with honest and well-respected partners (real-estate agents, title representatives, insurance agents, and home inspectors), as well as creating long-term win-win relationships with homebuyers and home sellers. Loan officers who understand the attitudes and objectives needed for successful team dynamics may be able to significantly increase their volume via long-term referral relationships. The formation of an effective and timely communication system informing homebuyers, home sellers, and team members of delays, transaction statuses, and concerns during the loan process positively impacts future business and referrals. The establishment of an honest communication system between loan officers and their team members will develop interdependency, creating a long-term, mutually beneficial relationship.

Keys to create successful referral relationships include:

1. Communication
2. Timely status reports
3. Honesty
4. Integrity
5. Caring and desire to help others
6. Time management
7. Knowledge of loan programs
8. Focus on results
9. Assume accountability

Communication is the key. If there is not a timely and effective communication line among your team members, you're doomed to fail. Create a timely system to update your real-estate partners, always act with the highest integrity, and show genuine concern for your clients. They are making one of the biggest purchases of their lives, many buying a home for the first time; understanding their apprehensiveness and concerns while acting in their best interest will contribute to a happy customer. Communication is the key to preparing your customers for possible delays or issues that may arise during the loan process. Properly informing team members and clients throughout the mortgage transaction process should allow all parties to properly prepare for unexpected issues that may arise.

Create a plan for communication. Weekly transaction status reports via e-mail and weekly phone calls to mortgage partners are effective ways to build your relationships. Unfortunately, many mortgage professionals avoid routine calls to others involved in the real-estate transaction and often delay contacting their real-estate partners and clients when problems arise during the transaction. Stand out from the crowd; create a plan of regular communication with your real-estate partners. Create a plan of contact points throughout the process with listing agents, selling agents, and your client. Relationship 101 teaches that mutual respect is built on honesty, caring, reliability, and communication. In the mortgage business, you also have to throw in knowledge. Develop your plan to cultivate relationships and grow your business. Loan officers who have been licensed for years may be able to reestablish lost relationships, and newly licensed loan officers may be able to create long-term interdependency through understanding what makes a happy customer.

BENEFITS OF BUSINESS RELATIONSHIPS

The benefits of personal relationships include contact with people who can help make you a success. You will have to offer your help to others, but you'll get plenty of rewards from your relationships also.

Below are examples of how relationship building can benefit you.

- * Advice, Experience, and Knowledge: If you're feeling lost or confused, turn to your network, someone with experience or expertise.

* Leads: If you're looking for new clients, it always pays to have someone who can give you some ideas of where to look.
* Word of Mouth: Many businesses will tell you that they get almost all of their business through referrals. These referrals can come from friends, family, and satisfied customers. It's a free and an effective way to promote yourself and generate more business.

HOW TO BUILD RELATIONSHIPS

Maintaining relationships will take care and effort; otherwise they will fade away. If you want to have strong relationships, you are going to have to pursue them and maintain them.

Follow these tips:

* Stay in touch to strengthen your relationships. You have to constantly work on maintaining your relationships. If you fail to stay in contact with someone, he or she may find someone else to partner with or may not immediately start to send you business and partner with you when you reach out. Send an e-mail or make a call weekly to stay in touch. If you forget to reach out to them or return their calls or e-mails, you will lose their business and they will find another loan officer who is more responsive.
* Relationships should be built on trust. Strong and sound relationships are win-win, where both parties are better off from the relationship. The key to building trust is

being honest. If you are willing to help your partners, your partners will know they can rely on you. Be dependable, and you'll create long-term successful relationships.
* Networking is a great way to create and build valuable relationships. Join the chamber of commerce, investor groups, or a nonprofit organization. Use social-media sites such as Facebook, LinkedIn, Twitter, Google, or Pinterest.
* Listen to your partners. One of the first steps in building a relationship is to show interest in other people. Listen to what people have to say. Keep track of what they have discussed in the past, and follow up with them. Everyone is impressed when someone shows he or she has taken the time to remember what is happening and what is important to him or her.
* Most business partners want to work with people who get results. You might need to show them you can deliver before you can expect them to have your back or send you referrals. It takes a lot of effort to build and maintain relationships.
* Always think about how you can help people in your network. They are far more likely to reciprocate with a referral than to give you a chance without working with you before.
* Focus on quality, not quantity. Be realistic about which relationships will help you grow your business. Don't stretch yourself too thin and create unnecessary work and aggravation for yourself.

Mistakes to Avoid

* Conversations should be more than business. Always remember that you are working on a mutually beneficial relationship. Be truthful and honest. Show your interest and concern in your potential networking partners' careers, families, and mutual interests.
* Show appreciation for your business partners' contributions and referrals. Make sure you acknowledge and appreciate their efforts. Do not forget to thank them.
* Update your networking relationships. If someone helps you find new business, keep that person updated on how he or she contributed to your success. This will demonstrate that you want a long-term relationship that is beneficial to both of you.
* Be consistent. In all your business and networking relationships, treat everyone with respect and be genuine. This will show you are honest, trustworthy, and reliable.
* Always be professional. Take responsibility, and do not blame others when problems arise. When a problem occurs, focus, keep the line of communication open, and resolve the problem as soon as possible. Resolving issues in a calm and professional manner builds character and shows others you are reliable and trustworthy.

* Be accountable. If you make a mistake, admit it and move on. Your partners and clients understand that mistakes are made, but lying about them can cause permanent damage to your relationships.
* Be dependable and reliable. Show up at meetings on time, and keep your promises. Failing to follow through with your commitments will cost your business and networking relationships. Your word is your bond. If your partners do not believe you, they will not send you their valuable clients, friends, and family.

Relationships take a lot of time and effort to build, but they can quickly be damaged or destroyed.

Relationships are essential to the sustained success of a mortgage loan officer. Work closely with people, and develop a rapport with them. Just make sure you always work on win-win relationships where both parties achieve greater success.

SALES CALLS (IN PERSON AND BY PHONE)

Even with the use of social media, mailings, phone calls, texts, and all the other ways you can contact individuals to grow your business, the face-to-face sales call is still the most powerful. Most real-estate agents, insurance brokers, attorneys, and other mortgage professionals are inundated by forms of non-face-to-face contact. Face-to-face contact is an essential part of expanding and keeping your current lead system. Before you meet with your current lead sources, you should prepare by following these simple suggestions.

* Gather information: The more you learn about your networking or business partners, the better prepared you will be when you meet them. Look on their social-media sites and talk to individuals who know both you and your lead source. Do you have similar interests? If you find out that they have recently been recognized for their business achievements, congratulate them on their success. The more information you have, the better the chance they'll want to do business with you. Do they have a need for specialized loan product for which you are an expert? What are their goals? Also, who do they currently use for their mortgage needs?
* Prepare: Once you have gathered valuable background information on your potential networking partner, you should write down the most important information so you can clearly discuss it in your face-to-face meeting. It may be your personal background, your loan product specialty, or similar interests or involvements you have. Tell the potential partner how you can make a difference in his or her business and the value to be gained by doing business with you.
* Set an appointment: Show your potential partners that you value them and their time. Set an appointment to talk to them. Do not just show up at their

office unexpectedly and ask to see them. Successful people in real estate, law, and insurance are extremely busy and have little time to waste. Show them that you value their business and their time.

* Be clear about your intentions: After you introduce yourself and are comfortable in the meeting, you should explain why you want to meet with your potential partner and discuss your goals. You may explain to him or her that you work with other people in his or her office or other people he or she has done business with and have had a lot of success. You may want to review the loan products you specialize in and how your service will benefit the potential partner. Ask him or her what his or her objectives and goals are and what he or she is looking for in a loan officer.
* Listen: Once your potential partner begins to talk about what he or she is looking for in a loan officer, give him or her as much time as necessary to explain how you can help. If he or she tells you how you can help, it will also tell you how you can earn his or her business.
* Follow up: Once you have started doing business with your new business partner, you will need to maintain the relationship. Constant contact is necessary to ensure you do not lose his or her future business. On a regular basis, you will need to call, e-mail, mail, and meet your lead partner face-to-face. Keep him or her updated on your joint transactions and whether there are any problems you need to resolve. This will show

your commitment to your partner and your value to outstanding customer service.

Pride yourself on being a highly skilled communicator and an expert in reading body language, as well as have well-developed questioning, listening, and assertiveness skills.

CUSTOMER-SERVICE SKILLS

Successful face-to-face sales involve a variety of competencies. They include timeliness, reliability, courtesy, knowledge of your products, and empathy. These behaviors need to be delivered in a sincere, enthusiastic, and friendly manner.

* Ask for referrals. Asking your existing and past clients to introduce you to those in their network is a great way to grow your business. This is particularly easy to do when a client has just had a good experience with you. While congratulating him or her on his or her success, you can simply ask, "Do you know of anyone else who may need a mortgage or have questions about refinancing their home?" Hopefully, he or she will give you the name and phone number of a friend or family member who may need your services or even take the time to introduce you, to make the initial contact easier.
* Make sure you thank your clients for any and all referrals. When someone in your network or a past customer refers a client lead to you, you should show

your appreciation by promptly sending a thank-you card. Always take the time and extend the effort to let that person know how much you appreciate him or her as a customer, even if it does not lead to a transaction in the future. If he or she does send you a referral, you could send a thank-you note or gift card. Everyone enjoys receiving a thank-you note or a gift of appreciation. Your thoughtful response to the referral will keep you on the client's mind if he or she has another friend or client who needs your services.

You must focus your attention on delivering outstanding service for your customers. By adding these simple strategies, you can enjoy an endless flow of quality potential customers in need of your mortgage expertise.

1. Make a list of people you know or want to know who can become your business partners.
2. Ask your existing customers for referrals of their friends and family you may be able to help.

Excellent customer service is crucial to the success of your lead-generation system. Just because you give good customer service, it doesn't mean you will get a lot of referrals. Receiving referrals on an ongoing basis is as much a function of deliberate planning as it is great customer service. Many small-business owners assume that referrals will happen by themselves if you give good customer service. If you are not proactive in asking for and creating referral[s...] you receiving as many referrals as you want are[...] remember, many of your most loyal customers a[nd] partners are ready and willing to give you referrals.

Creating a steady stream of referrals starts w[ith] attitude.

How do you get more referrals? You have to ask them. In reality, most loan officers know they have to ask fo[r] referrals to get more referrals, but the fear of rejection stops them from asking. If you provided outstanding service and the homebuyer is delighted with you, he or she will want to refer his or her friends and family to you. Happy customers want to give you referrals. It makes them feel good that they found a great loan officer they had a good experience with, and they will want to help their friends and family by referring you to them. When their friends receive great service from you as well, your referring customers will feel as though they were able to do their friends a great favor. Always ask for a referral, if you have treated that person the way you would expect to be treated. Believe in yourself and the value of your experience and knowledge as a mortgage professional.

There are two sources for referrals: your current customers and leads from your sphere of influence. You should have an active referral system for both types of people. Your customers are perhaps your most enthusiastic referrers because they have experienced your product. But you may in fact get more referrals from other influential people who have never for obtaining referrals from other influential ... program with your ... absolutely critical. ... not institutionaliz... ...y confuse word-... system and overlook the ...using for loan officers. Develop ...ills and referral programs and start ben-... an endless stream of new customers.

HOW TO DEVELOP REFERRAL SOURCES

The word-of-mouth referral is the least expensive but most effective way to new high-quality clients. The fewer degrees of separation between the loan officer and the client will result in a higher comfort level for both parties. Get a referral from someone you know and trust, such as other loan officers, professionals, or contacts in the real-estate industry who share your approach to business and who are good referral prospects. Marketing to and with referral sources will result in new business and a more rewarding working relationship.

Most importantly, though, a good referral program saves time, enriches your relationships, and minimizes hard marketing costs.

The keys to building and sustaining a good referral network are as follows:

* Identify qualified referral sources
* Take a long-term approach that focuses on relationship
* Understand needs and motives
* Take care of your referral sources

Every service-oriented company requires clients, and clients don't come any better than by referral.

A referral network can provide a good stream of business. Once you have demonstrated your value and managed relationships carefully, you can focus a significant portion of marketing time on keeping the network growing. But each individual is motivated to refer you work by different factors. Your goal is to understand people's motives and to respond and accommodate them to the best of your ability.

Some referral sources may view you as having the same potential to refer work to them. This is only a problem if you are unable to reciprocate. If you already have an insurance agent or a title company you send all your clients to, you need to find another way to increase your new referral partners' business.

Others may see you working for their clients as a benefit to their relationships, given your skill and expertise. A referral to a client who works out well reflects positively on his or her working relationship. Everyone wins, and the client stays within a trusted circle of professionals, receiving excellent service and advice.

Loan officers who maintain and grow their relationships by exceeding expectations with service, response, and knowledge align services and responses more closely to the client, resulting in both the referral source and client benefiting from your services.

When you receive referrals, there are two people to impress: the person who gave you the referral and the client. Never compromise your position of trust with the referral source; if so, you will risk future referrals from your referral source. Always keep your referral source updated on your progress, but be careful not to disclose any private details. Your discretion will be noted and appreciated.

Create a list of qualified referral sources.

Design and develop your referral network one person at a time. Who are the ideal professionals to influence prospective clients? Make a list of everyone you know or have been in contact with over the past twelve months.

Referral networks can include the following:

1. Real-estate agents
2. Lawyers
3. Insurance agents
4. Influential individuals
5. Business leaders
6. Contractors

Your marketing efforts should include specific plans to attract, educate, and motivate this target market. But are you in contact with the right group of people, such as influential people who are in dialogue with your potential clients? Are these individuals aware of your expertise and services?

Influential people should be well known, trustworthy, and reliable professionals in their industry. Take the time to identify potential referral partners. Ask yourself the following:

Who advises homebuyers before they contact me?

Who is targeting homebuyers but offers a different type of service?

Who influences homebuyers prior to looking for their next home?

Building quality referral sources takes time. Understand how to strengthen your relationships and bring value.

As with all your marketing efforts, define your target audience and understand their needs. Marketing to clients refers to the end users of your services, whereas marketing to an influential person refers to developing referral relationships for a continual stream of clients who need your mortgage services.

The list below includes suggestions on how to get to know and develop trust and partnership with individuals who have influence over potential new mortgage clients.

1. Seminar for the target audience.

Offer free seminars on your loan products or services. This will enable you to demonstrate your knowledge, specialization, and expertise on mortgage products. Suggest joint seminars where you both speak on your specialties and share in bringing clients to the seminar. This will show you are committed to a win-win relationship with your new influential partner.

2. Try to assist others in growing their businesses.
Write an article for their newsletter or website. Introduce them to your networking group.

If you are able develop referral lead sources that result in additional leads, then your all-encompassing marketing plan must include constant communication, expressions of gratitude, and reciprocated business to your lead partners.

Always take special care of your top referral lead sources. Appropriate the majority of your marketing efforts and time toward your top referral sources.

The following suggestions are ways you can show your gratitude to your top referral lead partners:

1. Provide outstanding customer service.
2. Be responsive and provide excellent communication.
3. Keep them informed—eliminate surprises.
4. Offer joint seminars to increase your sphere of influence and each of your business volumes.

Give special attention to individual referrals. A handwritten thank-you note, phone call, or a lunch meeting would be appropriate to show your gratitude.

Maintain regular contact with your referral source.

Increase referrals by encouraging past customers and your sphere of influence to recommend you through constant marketing.

Consistency is built upon developing long-term referral relationships.

Grow and maintain your sphere of influence to develop a consistent stream of referrals.

Here's how to grow your sphere of influence:

* Join and become active in organizations.
* Participate in real-estate events.
* Volunteer in your community.
* Provide great customer service.

Building and developing long-term relationships will bring continuous and profitable referral streams.

To provide outstanding customer service, you must keep the real-estate agents and buyers informed throughout the transaction. Let them know if delays occur and the timeframe needed to overcome the delay or issue. Your marketing system must include great customer service but also regular contact with your past customers and referral sources. The following suggestions will help you stay in contact with your sphere of influence:

* Personal newsletter with useful mortgage and real-estate information
* Thank-you cards after the mortgage closes
* Birthday and anniversary cards
* E-mail contact
* Phone calls
* Community involvement to show your clients you are invested in the community

As a loan officer, these suggestions will help you create stronger and lasting relationships with Realtors, maximize referrals from past customers, and develop a step-by-step plan to grow your sphere of influence.

A sound referral system is the foundation of your business. It is important to take the time to set up a formal system that generates leads and new business through referrals. Track your progress and determine which referral approaches are generating leads and new business. Focus on what works, and eliminate what is not working.

* Contact past customers. The lifeblood of most successful loan officers is repeat customers and referrals from satisfied customers.
* Join networking groups to build your referral outlets. New loan officers who are just starting to find referral partners should contact their local chamber of commerce, for-profit networking groups, and other business associations such as Kiwanis or Rotary for business referral partners.
* Always remember to ask your past customers, family, friends, and sphere of influence for referrals. Many past clients and individuals who know and trust you are more than willing to refer their friends and family. You have to ask for the referral. The best new customer is referred by a previous happy customer.
* Create a referral system you can stick to. Use monthly e-mails, phone calls, mailings, and holiday cards

to stay in touch with your sphere of influence. If you create a follow-up and referral system that you can manage and are comfortable with, you will be continually cultivating referrals.

* Social media is an inexpensive and effective marketing tool. Use social media as an outreach system to reach new clients and develop and grow your referral network, which should include your sphere of influence, past clients, and new clients. Social-networking sites such as LinkedIn, Facebook, Pinterest, and Google+ are all avenues to share your information with others. They will allow you to stay in touch with past customers, offer valuable information and advice, and grow your referral opportunities.

To be a successful loan officer, relationship building is key. There are many companies that offer Internet leads where you are being shopped by the customer. If you want to build long-term relationships, you will need to create a steady stream of potential clients who trust and respect you as a mortgage loan officer. The best new customer is a customer referred by a family member or friend. Creating loyalty through relationship building will create long-term success for mortgage loan officers. Success and consistency are founded in being diligent in your marketing efforts to your past customers and sphere of influence, which is crucial to your long-term success.

Once you have generated a referral and then preapproved the mortgage, you must then close the mortgage with effective communication and good customer service. The next step is to develop a long-term relationship with the listing and selling agent through timely contact and useful information. Without effective and useful communication, you will eventually lose the relationship with your past customer or real-estate partner. Focus on your sphere of influence and provide the best service you can for your customers and business partners. If the average person moves every seven years and you have 350 past customers, that means you should have fifty leads in your sphere of influence every year who need your services. This number does not consider their friends or family members who could refer you or if rates fall and there is a refinance boom. After just a few years in the mortgage business, the value of your past-customer database is immense. Past customers should consider you as their expert in the mortgage business. There should be trust and mutual understanding; this is the best type of business you can generate and maintain.

START WITH YOUR SPHERE OF INFLUENCE (RELATIONSHIP BUILDING)

Who makes up your sphere of influence? Think of people in the following categories: past customers, friends, relatives, friends of family, licensed real-estate agents, escrow officers, other lenders, insurance agents, business contacts, coworkers from previous jobs, neighbors, CPAs or tax preparers, and chamber of commerce members. The list should be as long as you can make it. Think of anyone you have a relationship with and see on a regular or scheduled basis. Chances are many of these individuals will need your services at some point, or they should at least be able to refer you to their friends or family.

After identifying your sphere of influence and developing relationships with them, focus on building lasting relationships with the ones you believe will refer your business and help grow your business.

Developing, growing, and maintaining relationships are the key to long-term success.

You must consistently contact your sphere of influence. Stay in touch with your clients and build lasting relationships. Use social media, direct calls, and consistent mailings as an effective tool to grow sales and profit and to stay in touch with them. You must present yourself as an expert and the go-to person in the mortgage business. When they call, you should answer their questions and help them to the best of your abilities, even if they do not need a mortgage or your services at that time.

Your marketing system should contact everyone in your sphere of influence at least once every six weeks for them to remember. Be their go-to person with any mortgage-related questions. E-mailing useful information and sending a different postcard every other month is a great way of staying in contact with your lead sources, showing that you are available and ready to help them when they have questions. Sending a constant stream of e-mails and postcards and mixing in an occasional phone call will make you the first name they think of when the time comes for a mortgage professional. Focusing on your sphere and then adding new contacts to your lead source list you will help your business grow and thrive.

You have to learn how to master your business. Become a walking encyclopedia of mortgage information. You should be able to recite the guidelines for the main mortgage products and know how to answer questions about the interstices that have derailed loans from receiving approval. If your friends, family, or sphere of influence have mortgage-related questions, you should be the first person they think of for help. When you are the expert and couple your knowledge with a philosophy of outstanding customer service, you will receive referrals and leads from the full spectrum of individuals you have come in contact with.

Create a system based on knowledge, helping others, communication, and great customer service. Once you have developed a relationship that produces a stream of referrals, maintain and cultivate it. Your best relationships may come from any source, including past customers, friends, business partners, or acquaintances from volunteer organizations. Your follow-up system should be based on staying in touch with all your past customers and business partners.

KEEPING YOUR PAST CUSTOMERS FOR LIFE

Most loan officers consider their past customers as the focal point of their business. Once you have been in the mortgage profession for three or four years, the majority of your business should be generated from your past customers. You should look for more than refinance opportunities from your past clients. They should also provide you with referrals of their friends and family, contact you when they want to purchase another house or want to refinance, and refer other professionals to you who are in related businesses to the mortgage business.

HOW TO NURTURE AND BUILD YOUR BUSINESS

Focus on the needs of your customers. Don't always toot your own horn on how great and knowledgeable you are in the mortgage profession. Listen to your customers. Tell them how you can meet their wants and needs in mortgage financing. If they have credit issues, are self-employed, or have other issues that make mortgage financing hard to obtain, explain how you can help them or provide a game plan on what they can do to prepare for a mortgage in the future, along with a realistic timeframe. Show them you are there for the long run and you will help them during their path to financing their next home. Smile and be pleasant.

If you are too businesslike and cold, the customers will notice, and your relationship will eventually end. Long-term relationships will be more fruitful and often provide leads and future business. Always be positive, even if stressful situations arise. Positive interaction will defuse customers who are upset.

Become involved in the community to create a greater reach for your business services. Invite fellow business professionals to partner with you in your marketing efforts and create win-win lead sharing partnerships.

HOW TO CULTIVATE EXISTING CUSTOMERS

Existing customers are the backbone to your business. You should have a plan to make sure they contact you and refer you for future mortgages. Create a plan to stay in touch with your past customers. Timely contact will keep you in front of them for their and their family and friends' future mortgage needs.

MAINTAIN CUSTOMER SATISFACTION

One of the most important elements in business is to create satisfied customers. Being polite will make you a lot easier to deal with. Always strive to provide good customer service and timely communication. Recognize people who help you, and say thank you to your lead-generation partners and customers. Most satisfied customers will tell a few of their friends and family, whereas unhappy customers will tell everyone who will listen.

Resolve customer problems and disputes. Your reputation is your greatest asset. Your business will grow simply by maintaining and helping your current customers.

Communication with your customers should be helpful to them, providing useful information regarding refinance, cash out, equity loan, or investment mortgage information. If you work for a mortgage broker and he or she sells the mortgages to a mortgage servicer, make sure you let your past customers know that they may receive solicitations from their mortgage servicer, but you are there to help them if they have any future mortgage needs or questions.

Always ask for referrals. In the mortgage business, a referral from a past customer is the best and least expensive way to create new business. It also is the best acknowledgment that you have provided great customer service and had a very satisfied customer. When a loan you have worked on transfers and funds, you should call both the selling and listing real-estate agents and the homebuyer and congratulate them on the purchase and transfer of the home. At this point, you should also ask them if they know of anyone who is thinking of purchasing a house or may need to refinance. The day the loan closes and the property transfers is the best time to ask for a referral. You should also follow up your phone call with a handwritten thank-you note congratulating the buyer on the purchase of his or her house and thanking each real-estate agent for working with you to assist the buyer in the purchase of the new house. Take this opportunity to ask for referrals.

Effective customer retention is the backbone to long-term success as a mortgage loan officer. Many loan officers receive 50 percent or more of their business annually from past customers. Past customers' loyalty results in new purchases or refinance or past customers referring their friends or family. Therefore, loyal customers are a vital part of your success.

THE IMPORTANCE OF CUSTOMER SERVICE

From the initial meeting, during the loan process, and after the mortgage transfers are all key points of contact for great customer service. Great customer service is the number-one key to retaining, maintaining, and earning new leads. Customer service is the key component to maintaining and generating income and increasing profitability. Your customers' perception of how you have handled the overall loan process will affect their opinion of you and your company. Future business from your clients will also rely on their perception of how they were treated during the loan process. Providing good customer service and timely communication is the lifeblood of your business. It is important to listen to customers and know what is important to them, thereby showing them that they are important and you value their business. Providing timely updates and an open line of communication will create a relationship built on trust and will allow greater leeway if there are problems during the transaction.

Your relationships with your customers should be built on trust. If there is a delay or problems occur, make sure you keep them informed. Let them know what happened and how it will affect the mortgage and if their closing could be delayed. Even though they may be upset, open and timely communication will allow them to prepare and inform other parties to the transaction. Let them know if you need any additional documentation and how you intend to solve the problem. Although they may be upset, they will appreciate the explanation and clear communication on their transaction. Always keep your customers informed. Hiding problems and delays from your clients will only create a trust issue and create animosity in your relationship.

Keep them informed and explain that you are working for them and in their best interest. Most individuals will appreciate your candor, and once the mortgage files, you may have created a customer who sings your praises to his or her friends and family. Even if you had to overcome problems, as long as you resolved them and kept your client updated, he or she will probably become a customer of yours for life. Homebuyers who have negative experiences will not only be lost as future customers but will also tell all their friends and family how horrible their experience was, even if you had little to do with the issues on their mortgage. Even worse, they may post their experience on social-media sites. If this happens, you may want to contact the past client and thoroughly explain the issue and how you tried to resolve the problems. Many times he or she will understand that the other parties involved in the transaction had a hand in the delays. Communication is always the best option. Some customers will just not want to discuss what happened or change their mind on their experience; try to explain what occurred and make them happy. If they are still unhappy, listen to what they have to say, move on, and accept what happened. Always treat your customers will respect. Sales and the mortgage business sometimes require a thick skin. Sometimes you will get blamed for something out of your control.

You can promote yourself through the following means from outstanding customer service.

- * Testimonials—After the mortgage has filed and the buyers have moved into their new home, assuming they have had an excellent experience, ask them for a testimonial you could share to promote yourself and share with future homebuyers. If marketed properly, this will increase your visibility with your sphere of influence and create more positive exposure for your business.
- * Higher Income_As you excel in the art of great customer service, more of your past customers will share their home-buying experience with their friends and family and help advertise your services by word-of-mouth marketing and social media. The amount of leads you receive will increase exponentially. As long as your interest rates and loan products are in line with the competition, you will earn most of their business thanks to your customer-service skills. This will result in greater profitability per transaction and higher income for you.
- * Motivation—The happier your clients are, the more motivated they will be to tell their family and friends. If you received a phone call, note, or posting on social media praising you for their experience during the mortgage process, it'll be extremely motivating to you. Happy customers will equate to greater job

satisfaction and performance. This will increase your sense of pride and motivation to do an even better job for your clients in the future.

The benefits of good customer service were meant to help you understand more about why treating your customers with care is extremely important. By practicing excellent customer service on a consistent basis, you will be able to help your business grow in a way that provides increased exposure and visibility regarding the services you provide for your homebuyers. When an individual has closed a mortgage with your company and feels that he or she has received the best possible service, he or she will likely share the experience, which will result in greater referrals, loyal clients, and increased profitability.

Chapter 4

CUSTOMER SERVICE
REPEAT BUSINESS

Repeat sales are created from exceptional customer service, staying in contact with your past customers and your sphere of influence. To create a long-term business relationship, you develop these relationships over time. Thank-you notes, anniversary cards, and birthday e-mails are just a few ways to stay in touch. Making the customers feel appreciated and needed is how you maintain your relationship.

BUILDING YOUR REPUTATION

If your business is based on excellent customer service and communication, you will undoubtedly build an outstanding reputation in the mortgage industry. Your sphere of influence, which includes past customers and partners, will speak of you as an expert and a partner they can rely on to close the loan on time and also make them look good. The best advertisement you can get is for your customers and partners to talk about their experiences with you. Providing outstanding customer service will allow your clients to tell their friends and family how happy they were with their experience in obtaining a mortgage from you. This will result in a significant increase in business. Conversely, poor customer service will destroy your partnerships and severely limit referrals from your clients. Great customer service is the backbone to success in the mortgage industry.

ELEMENTS OF EXCELLENT CUSTOMER SERVICE

You may not always have the lowest rate or every loan product that your competitors offer, but by providing excellent customer service, you can limit the amount of customers you lose to your competition.

FINDING YOUR NICHE

Many loan officers specialize in loan products such as credit repair, first-time homebuyer down-payment-assistance products, or rehabilitation loans. The obvious niche for future success is customer service and communication. Even if you have problems with a particular loan, it is imperative that you communicate with your customer and your partners about the issues you are having. Set yourself apart from your competition. Make it a priority to keep everyone informed of the loan progress and aware of any delays or issues you are experiencing. It is critical in today's environment that you meet closing dates and contractual obligations; if delay occurs, you must keep everyone informed and ask them for assistance in resolving the issues.

The following is a list of how outstanding customer service can positively impact your future business.

* Word-of-Mouth Marketing—The best way to promote yourself is through word-of-mouth marketing. When you deliver exceptional customer service, you will likely receive praise from your clients and business partners to their friends and through their use of social media.
* Increasing Your Sphere of Influence—Excellent customer service will expand your reach and allow you to obtain additional clients through your past customers and partners. Their word-of-mouth marketing will help you stand out from your competition.
* Testimonials—When you provide outstanding customer service, it is in your best interest to seek out customer feedback. You can promote yourself through social media and other marketing efforts with testimonials from past customers. Also, it will provide you an outlet to improve as a loan

officer. Understanding your strengths and weaknesses is the fastest way to meet your customers' expectations.
* Ultimate Customer Satisfaction—Happy customers will lead to increased business and higher income.

FOLLOWING THE TRANSACTION

The mortgage industry has always been reactionary. Most mortgage professionals do not keep their clients and their partners updated on the loan progress. Usually the clients and real-estate agents call the loan officers for updates. When problems arise and delays happen, this causes severe dissatisfaction with the loan officer and the mortgage company. It is all too common for real-estate agents or clients to state that they get little to no feedback on their loan progress and feel that they are left in the dark on what is happening with their mortgage. Taking the position of being proactive through communication, both verbally (phone calls) and via e-mail, shows the customer you're trying to keep them updated of where they are in the loan process. By doing so, if delays or problems occur, at least the customer will feel you are working in his or her best interest to keep him or her updated and are reaching out for help in a timely manner. Keeping the customer and real-estate agent informed on a regular basis throughout the loan process will greatly increase your customer-service level.

KEEPING ALL PARTIES INFORMED

Effective communication is a critical component of outstanding customer service. Your communication efforts should be focused to ensure excellent service to your clients and real-estate agents and partners, as well as a way to quickly resolve any issues that may arise. In dealing with your clients, open and clear communication is essential, whether it is face-to-face, over the phone, or by e-mail.

FOR BEST CUSTOMER SERVICE
Communication Is Key

Understanding how to communicate effectively allows the loan officer to properly respond to the homebuyers' concerns and relates to the issues occurring with the mortgage loan. It is imperative that the homebuyer understands what is happening in his or her loan, where he or she is in the loan process, what to expect, and whether the closing date is delayed. Follow-up during the loan process with all parties involved, including the homebuyer, the mortgage-company support staff, the listing and selling agents, and the title company is vital to effectively controlling the loan process. Even if the closing expectations cannot be met due to an unforeseen circumstance, effective communication will likely defuse the homebuyers' and real-estate agents' frustration.

If a problem or delay occurs during the loan process, depending on the severity of the issue, a highly stressful situation may arise from the homebuyer or real-estate agent's frustration and anxiety. In a situation, such as this it is important to be able to go to your sales manager or underwriting manager to help defuse it.

Implementing avenues of constant follow-up will help show the customer in your real-estate partners your commitment to providing the best customer service possible. The tools you can use for follow-up include face-to-face communication, phone calls, e-mails, mailings, thank-you cards, balloons, holiday cards, and birthday cards.

SET CLEAR EXPECTATIONS WITH YOUR CUSTOMERS

Be proactive; you have to take the time up front to tell the customer what will happen during the loan process. If he or she does not know what to expect, there will be frustration, and he or she will seek advice from friends or the real-estate agent for advice. This will lead to buyer frustration. If you clearly describe the loan process, set expectations up front, and tell homebuyers what they need to do at each point, there will be much less frustration during the process. In addition, you must set follow-up expectations with your customers.

KEEP EVERYONE UPDATED

As you reach major milestones during the loan process, you should contact your partners and the customer to inform them. This would include, at a minimum, the appraisal, survey, title commitment issuance, and underwriting. If a problem arises, contact the customer first and then your business partner and inform both of how this issue can be handled.

Don't wait; if they find out before you call them, it will be much harder to handle the issue.

BE PROACTIVE

There are many opportunities throughout the year to contact your past customers. These include the anniversary of the purchase of the house, customer(s) birthday, birth of a child, holidays, or opportunities for them created by the mortgage market. Use these opportunities to stay in touch with your customers. Know when to be formal and when to be casual when communicating with your customers. Once you know the customers, it will be in the best interest to communicate on a first-name basis, to create a friendly communication stream.

What is the right number of contacts annually for a past customer? The goal is to establish a long-term relationship with your customer. You will need to contact your past customers on a regular basis based on the mortgage-market conditions. In a regular year, you should schedule eight to ten contact points with your past customers. But if there is a reason to call them—for example, if interest rates have fallen and it is in their best interest to refinance or they have told you that they will be purchasing another house or an investment property—take the opportunity to stay in contact to help them with their housing goals. The goal is to show your past customers they're special and that you want to help in the future.

EXCEED EXPECTATIONS

When you are contacted by your past customer or any customer, it is in your best interest to try to go above and beyond his or her expectations. When you qualify him or her for a loan, be thorough with your answer about what the options are. If he or she has credit or life issues that will prevent him or her from getting a loan at that time, you should take the time to let him or her know what he or she needs to do to resolve the issues and how much time it will take.

HOW TO CREATE SATISFIED CUSTOMERS

Satisfied customers can be a strategy you use to acquire and retain more customers. Always be honest and inform specific customers what to expect. Try to exceed expectations and advise them of any delays or problems as soon as they occur. Take the attitude that the transaction is not complete until the customer is satisfied.

BENEFITS OF QUALITY CUSTOMER SERVICE

Prevents Some Future Problems—If complaints are solved quickly, they will likely not become major problems that are time-consuming and costly to resolve.

Retaining Existing Customers—Future sales and referrals are typically lost through poor follow-up and service.

Quality Service and Follow-Up— Great service is created through effective communication and constant follow-up with all parties to the mortgage transaction. Great service is the only way to overcome higher cost.

Think of each customer as your only account, and when responding, think of how you would like to be treated if you were going through the loan process as a homebuyer.

Just remember that retaining a customer is much easier and less expensive than finding a new customer. Anticipate issues and try to resolve them before they become major problems.

Even if one of your customers has issues on a transaction or is delayed in closing, most will become repeat customers and refer their friends and family if handled properly. The key is to address the issue, keep the customer informed, and resolve the issue as quickly as possible. Show the customer he or she is important, that you value him or her as a client, and you are trying to resolve the issue.

Follow-up is crucial during the transaction. Keep the customer and the Realtors informed. Take personal responsibility for your transaction. Do not make excuses; take responsibility.

After you fund and close a mortgage, always call the buyer and real-estate agents involved and congratulate them on successfully closing the transaction. Congratulate the new homebuyer on closing on the new home. You also need to ask yourself the following questions: Were the buyer and Realtors involved in the transaction happy with your service? Did you provide outstanding customer service to all parties involved in the transaction and keep everyone informed in contact with your sphere of influence? Did you handle and resolve any problems to the best of your ability? If the buyer or one of the Realtors criticized part of the transaction, did you listen and try to improve from that input? Did you let all parties know that you enjoyed working with them and are more than happy to help any of their family, friends, or other individuals that they may know who may be in need of a mortgage in the near future?

PAST-CUSTOMER TESTIMONIALS AND ENDORSEMENTS (BRAG BOOK)

Social media, such as Facebook, Twitter, LinkedIn, and other ways to reach potential customers, provides an inexpensive but important marketing tool. It is a great and inexpensive way to share information, keep potential homebuyers informed of loan product guideline changes, and show your expertise in mortgage lending.

THE VALUE OF CUSTOMER TESTIMONIALS

The most powerful marketing tool is a personal referral or testimonial. When buying a house, or applying for a mortgage, most individuals value input from their friends and family. The use of past-customer testimonials is one of the most effective and powerful forms of advertising. After you close a mortgage, you should send your customer a thank-you for his or her business. At that time, ask for a reference or testimonial of his or her experience. These are great marketing pieces that you can use to create flyers and mailings, use in your newsletter, and put on social media for future customers to read.

Chapter 5

SOCIAL MEDIA AND OTHER LEAD SOURCES

How to Generate Mortgage Leads.

The following suggestions are avenues to lead generation.

Networking—Join business groups, clubs, and organizations where you can give as well as receive additional business. Your personal network would consist of your family, friends, and acquaintances who may need mortgage financing. Market to this group of individuals, and keep them informed of your loan products, changes, and rates. At some point they may want to purchase a house, refinance, improve their house, or buy an investment property. They may also have friends or family they can refer to you as customers. Let them know that you appreciate their help in growing your business and that if they need help growing their business, you intend to reciprocate by sending them potential leads.

Real-Estate Community—Continually make face-to-face sales calls, regularly make phone calls, and mail informational pieces; use social media, e-mail advertising, lunch meetings, and joint presentations to collaboratively generate business. Even if you are an expert, you will need to show the real-estate agent that partnering with you will generate more business for him or her. If you don't succeed at first, keep trying. With persistence, you will eventually be given an opportunity. Show you're knowledgeable and willing to provide great customer service to earn repeat business.

Many loan officers and Realtors jointly advertise on social-media sites. Loan officers often provide open-house financing sheets and yard signs, sit with Realtors at open houses, and provide food at brokers' opens. These are all avenues to meet new real-estate agents and grow your sphere of influence in the real-estate community.

Social-Media Marketing—Set up a personal website that will generate mortgage leads. Post ads on websites and blogs, use yard signs, and take out advertisements in newspapers as well as local trade publications.

Use the power of the Internet to advertise your service. Online mortgage forums, e-mail marketing, pay-per-click, and banners are all great forms of lead generation. Be sure to offer a variety of ways to contact you for advice or to solicit leads from the Internet.

Write an article and have it published in local real-estate magazines. This is an effective way to gain familiarity in the local real-estate community. Mail out flyers or postcards advertising the products you specialize in. The more specialized the niche, the better to attract interest.

Participate in trade shows to create new mortgage leads. Set up a booth at a home-improvement trade show and advertise your mortgage products and services. You may want to advertise products such as refinance, cash-out refinance, rehabilitation, or home-equity products that will allow homeowners to pull equity out of their homes.

You could also purchase leads from a mortgage-lead-generation company. Before you purchase any leads, it is important to verify that they have not been sold to other mortgage brokers. Be sure to ask the lead-generation company about their guarantee and return policy. At first purchase only a few leads, so you can verify firsthand if they are of good quality. Are the buyers or refinancers able to be financed, given their equity positions and credit scores? When you are on the phone with customers, ask them when they submitted their mortgage information inquiry and if any other lender has contacted them.

Use the Multiple Listing Service (MLS) to create a list of recently listed properties. You should be able to access the listing agent's information and the owner of the listed properties' contact information through the online white pages. With this information, you should be able to contact the listing agents to see if you can help them with financing sheets for their listed properties, open houses, or brokers' opens, or to qualify potential buyers for the properties. Also, ask them if the seller of the property intends to purchase another house.

Ask permission to contact the seller if they say the he or she intends to purchase another house.

Call, e-mail, and mail the sellers with mortgage program information about you and your company.

When mortgage companies use social media to reach new customers, they have to comply with numerous regulations and maintain an audit trail. Make sure you notify your sales manager of all your social-media marketing as a loan officer. On all social-media advertising, you will need to disclose the following information: your name, contact information, state, NMLS license numbers, and your company and branch NMLS numbers. The Internet will allow you as a mortgage professional to reach potential borrowers through Facebook, LinkedIn, and Twitter. Social media is an inexpensive way to find and help homebuyers quickly.

Prior to advertising on social media, make sure you discuss your social-media marketing with your company. There are numerous regulations for any social-media efforts by financial institutions.

The following are suggestions on how to use social media as a marketing tool.

CREATE YOUR OWN CONTENT

If you're using social networks to promote yourself, it is best to create your own content. Create your own blog, and link all your posts on social-media sites back to your own personal blog. Educational and informational posts are usually the most beneficial for mortgage loan officers. Track your traffic and determine which posts and content create the greatest response.

If someone replies to information you post online, make sure you thank that person. Also, if someone writes a review about you and your service and posts it on the Internet, make sure you contact that person to show him or her you are concerned with your image and care about the service you provide to your clients.

As a loan officer, you can help your business grow and be more profitable and successful through a variety of social-media outlets. But you need to learn how to do this first. Understand that you have the ability to influence others through content that is informative, creative, and engaging. Always take the approach of helping others first, and you will find success on social-media sites.

When most people consider buying a big-ticket item such as their first house, buying a second home, or a mortgage to refinance their home, they seek advice from their friends and family. They ask their friends and coworkers for names and phone numbers of reputable loan officers and inquire whether they have recently gone through the mortgage process. A direct referral from someone they know is more powerful than a cold advertisement. Hearing from someone they trust regarding a recent pleasant experience is one of the best forms of marketing you can receive.

SOCIAL MEDIA

The use of social media by your customers is a free electronic form of word-of-mouth advertising. It reaches a greater number of people at a faster rate than traditional word-of-mouth advertising.

ENCOURAGING YOUR CUSTOMERS TO USE SOCIAL MEDIA

Most of your customers use social media; they share their activities and events on a variety of websites to stay in touch with their friends. Therefore, encouraging them to share their home-buying and mortgage experience should be fun and exciting for them. Friend them on their social-media site and share their comments, posts, and testimonials about your mortgage services and products.

YOUR CUSTOMERS CAN PROMOTE YOU ON SOCIAL MEDIA

The more satisfied and happy customers you have regarding their home-buying experience, the greater the chance they will share their experience with their friends and connections on social media. You will need to ask them to share their homebuyer journey on social media as a means to reach more clients. Social media is an inexpensive way to access a large group of potential customers. Your past customers can create warm leads for you by sharing their positive experience with you and your mortgage company. Their social-media posts are a referral source for individuals considering buying a home or refinancing. The home-buying experience is long and often emotional, so if your customers have a good experience in obtaining their mortgage, they will be more than happy to share this major life event with others. Encouraging them to share their home-buying experience is a key component to your marketing activity.

SOCIAL MEDIA IS PART OF THE MARKETING PUZZLE

Your marketing budget and the forms of marketing that you engage in will need to be all-encompassing. You will need to part take in a variety of marketing, networking, direct mailings, e-mails, and social-media advertising to reach your clients. Social media is the perfect form of outreach because almost all individuals engage in some social media, and it is one of the least expensive forms of advertising. Social-media advertising will add that extra boost to your marketing efforts, allowing you to reach your customers, their contacts, real-estate/mortgage/title professionals, and a variety of audiences who are in need of your services.

Consumer reviews, testimonials, opinions, and ratings are all part of advertising in today's world. The faster you embrace it and use it to your advantage, the faster you will grow and control your business. Just remember, you will need as many good reviews and comments as possible. One bad review can impact your business as much as ten good reviews. You should seek out feedback and testimonials from satisfied and happy customers to promote yourself. Try to interact with your customers and potential customers on a regular basis on social media. If you have an unhappy customer, you should try to make him or her happy or at least give him or her a better understanding of what happened during the transaction that caused issues or delays. Clear communication is sometimes the best you can offer in the mortgage banking profession.

HOW TO BUILD CREDIBILITY WITH SOCIAL MEDIA

Consumers want to do business with knowledgeable and experienced loan officers. Social media is the perfect tool to help past customers and homebuyers find you and your services. Social media and the content you post and provide to potential customers will help you gain credibility and be deemed as an expert in mortgage financing. You will become the go-to person for answers with their mortgage questions. They will seek out your advice and knowledge, thereby creating a stream of leads for new mortgage loans.

POSITION YOURSELF AS AN EXPERT

Use social media to build your credibility as an expert in mortgage financing. The first step is to post content (preferably original) on social media that is helpful to homebuyers. The information should be useful to homebuyers, not merely marketing pieces. As an expert, you should post information and tips on particular mortgage programs, showing that you have specialized in a certain mortgage type, but you should also occasionally post general information that may be useful to all homebuyers. Your posts should be useful and relevant to the current mortgage and real-estate market. When rates are moving up or down, new down-payment assistance programs are created, or new mortgage products are released, you can use this content to keep your readers informed on market changes and opportunities. So, it is important to stay informed of news, governmental regulations, and market and mortgage product changes. You can also link information on recent changes to your social-media site to support your articles and informational pieces.

Take the approach that you are keeping individuals informed of changes and new opportunities in the real-estate market and mortgage industries. Be helpful in providing useful information to reach a far greater audience than just trying to sell your services as a mortgage lender.

If you are e-mailed questions, always try to answer the question thoroughly and provide useful information. Answering a question or resolving a problem may not lead to an immediate mortgage application but may create a stream of referrals because of your expertise and willingness to help others. Always try to provide a link or source for your response when possible. This will reinforce you and your expert status.

Chapter 6

HOW TO CREATE YOUR MARKETING/ADVERTISING BUDGET

Success as a loan officer requires a plan that focuses on your best characteristics and qualities. Once you have decided how to market yourself based on your best qualities, developing a business plan and deciding how much you can financially devote to your business are your next steps. Most loan officers devote at least 10 percent of their income toward their marketing/advertising budget. You must decide the minimum amount of money you can devote to your business monthly, and then when your business grows, you can increase your marketing budget accordingly. Your budget should include all your marketing activities, education, and personal assistants. The difference between success and failure is often as simple as following through on your plan consistently. If your sales are less than expected or if you are busier than expected, deviating from your advertising and marketing efforts will only create ups and downs in your business. Commitment to a continuous advertising and marketing plan is the key to your businesses success.

The following are category suggestions that can be included when creating your marketing budget: postage, Internet lead generation, print ads, dues and licensing, supplies, client gifts, flyers and brochures, and website expenses. You may also want to add an additional section titled "other" to cover unexpected expenses.

You should always be looking for cost-effective ways to advertise. The following are a few inexpensive suggestions: creating your own flyers and brochures, researching alternative publications for advertising, dropping off flyers instead of mailing, and using e-mail advertising as much as possible. Successful loan officers set aside at least 10 percent of their earnings for business expenses and advertising.

Steps to creating a living business/marketing plan:

* Thoroughly define your market, including any niche mortgage products you specialize in. Define how your knowledge and experience set you apart from your competition.
* Define your target clients and lead sources; include how your experience and expertise will provide better service. Explain how you can market your expertise and mortgage banking to your sphere of influence.

* Analyze your strengths (niche loan programs you are extremely knowledgeable in), weaknesses (loan programs, competitive pricing, etc.), and new or upcoming market opportunities (refinance, down-payment assistance programs, etc.). Ask yourself what loan types you are the most proficient in. Does your competition have programs you do not offer, is their pricing better, or are they able to close loans faster? In what ways do your processing, underwriting, and closing departments give you a competitive advantage over your competition? Maybe you can get loans approved regularly with lower credit scores. What are your processing, underwriting, and closing departments' weaknesses, and how will they affect your repeat and future business?
* Remember, you are selling service, convenience, expertise, and knowledge.
* What mortgage loan products are you the most knowledgeable in? Are your pricing, processing, or closing times better than your competition's on certain loan types? Do you intend to specialize in first-time homebuyers, second-time buyers, investors, the credit impaired, or individuals seeking rehabilitation mortgage products? How do you stand out from your competition, and how does your sphere of influence perceive you as a mortgage loan officer? This information will help you focus in on your target audience and marketing efforts.

* What are your weekly, monthly, and annual goals in originations? Your goals should be tracked and measured throughout the year so you can track and make changes to your business/marketing plan accordingly.
* Develop a marketing system that you can follow to reach your sphere of influence and networking partners to reach your sales and income goals. Incorporate any forms of advertising to reach your goals. These advertising sources may include direct calls, direct mail, social media, printed media, and networking. Current and past-customer contact systems should always be included as the basis for future business and referrals.
* Create and follow a detailed marketing budget. A marketing plan should be a continual function of your daily activities, focusing on creating and maintaining sales.
* Social media is an inexpensive tool that can be used to reach new customers as well as maintain existing relationships. Providing valuable information to potential customers will create opportunities for future business.

MARKETING PLAN

There are numerous ways to market yourself and your business. You should incorporate as many marketing outreach systems as possible. These marketing efforts may include word of mouth (past customers, friends, and family); purchased leads from real-estate partners and social media; print advertisements; letters and postcards to past customers; and referral sources (such as mortgage companies, banks, and title companies). Whichever marketing systems you incorporate into your plan, the greatest impact and most lasting results will come from building relationships. When you build relationships, you earn others' trust and will likely be referred to their sphere of influence when your services are needed.

First determine which marketing strategies you are going to implement, and create a daily, weekly, and monthly plan; how well you stick to the plan will determine your success. The most effective strategy is to stay in touch with past customers via phone calls, e-mails, newsletters, and holiday and birthday cards. Develop a follow-up system that keeps you in touch with your past customers. Eventually your efforts will pay off with referrals and repeat business. The key is to differentiate yourself from other mortgage loan officers. When your past customers think of buying another home, refinancing their current home, or starting home improvements, or when they hear a colleague or family member talking about buying or refinancing a home, you should be immediately thought of as the expert to contact. Referrals will multiply exponentially through the relationships of your past customers.

BUSINESS PLAN

You need to determine what income you will need to make consistently as a mortgage professional. Once you have determined the income you need monthly, you can then create a budget for your endeavors as a mortgage professional. Your budget should include all your expenditures for advertising, marketing, and education and the expected results from it. You need to be realistic with your expectations; increased loan production and profitability is a slow and methodical process. A 20 to 30 percent increase in business annually is a reasonable goal for a loan originator with three or more years' experience.

In order for loan officers to succeed, it is imperative to have a thoroughly thought-out business plan that considers market conditions and opportunities. The market and regulatory climate will undoubtedly impact your production and profitability.

BUSINESS PLAN TEMPLATE

Write a thorough summary of your objectives, including your customer-service expectations, income goals, and any achievements you would like to win, such as president's club, monthly sales leader, company trips, or other sales awards offered by your company. Write out the steps you intend to take to offer superior customer service (number of contacts throughout the process), focusing on the unique attributes you offer as a mortgage professional and to your clients and customers. You should also include your assistant's duties or, if you do not have an assistant, at what production level you will hire an assistant.

It is also beneficial to define what loan types you will offer and specialize in. Do you intend to offer standard loan products, such as conventional, FHA, and VA? Do you also want to offer FHA 203k rehabilitation loans, USDA, and reverse mortgages? Most successful loan officers specialize in one or two loan products and refer loans away if they are not knowledgeable on the loan product. Your posts and marketing content should focus on the loan types you intend to offer.

Develop a list of daily business objectives. Create a detailed daily activity chart to help you guide and manage your business.

Remember, your business plan is a living, breathing document that can change throughout the year as new opportunities arrive or doors close. Stay focused on building a profitable career as a mortgage loan officer. Be sure to track your performance as you follow the plan.

Projected loan volume (size and number) – You should monitor your sales on a weekly, monthly, and annual basis. Adjust your marketing efforts accordingly to achieve your goals.

Expected prequalification's – Keep track of the number of leads you are receiving from your sphere of influence. If you are not ore-qualifying enough potential buyers, you may have to increase your marketing efforts.

Expected lead-generation partners – Continually search for new partnerships to expand your business. New partners may offer higher quality buyers or larger sales volumes.

How to improve customer service and past-customer referral – Ask your partners and customers for feedback. Accept criticism and use the information to improve your service.

Offer new loan products – Although you should find a niche product to specialize in, you should be knowledgeable in new guidelines and products to reach and service a greater number of homebuyers.

Target new customers (first-time homebuyers, second-time buyers, investors, etc.)

Are rates falling or rising, new loan products, changing guidelines that may offer opportunities for new business.

Chapter 7

NETWORKING

Since most mortgage loan officers are fully or partially commissioned, it is important to treat your job as your personal business. How much income you make is dependent on how you market yourself and how many loans you close. Your business network is a type of social outlet for networking with other individuals who own complementary businesses. There are several national networking organizations that have created successful small-business networking groups. These networking groups offer small-business owners as well as loan officers the chance to create, develop, and build relationships to constantly generate opportunities to increase their lead sources and profitability.

For mortgage originators and small-business owners, this type of networking is typically a more cost-effective means of generating new business than other advertising, such as print or purchasing leads through social media. All referral systems, including business networking, are built upon long-term relationships that benefit both parties. Whether you join a national networking group or team up with local small-business owners to form your own networking partnerships, you should meet on a regular basis to reinforce your relationships and allow each member to promote him- or herself and exchange leads with other members. It is important that you find or form a group that has members who can become mutually beneficial to each party. For loan officers, a complementary relationship can be formed with real-estate agents, insurance agents, attorneys, and general contractors, to name a few.

The basic foundation in a successful business networking relationship is to connect like-minded business partners together who trust, benefit, and advertise for each another. Any successful long-term business networking is built on respect, trust, and belief that your business partner offers superior service or products. Your networking partner has to believe that your main goal is to help others and provide great service. Once you join or establish your networking group, it is important to attend meetings regularly as well as meet each member outside of the regular meetings consistently to strengthen your relationship and work together more effectively.

Your networking group should allow each member to give a presentation on his or her business or service to the other members on a rotating basis. Make sure the information you provide is professional and relevant to the other members. If the other members have questions about your business or service, thoroughly elaborate on your answers. A more detailed description of your business may help your networking partners provide additional leads to your business. Some of your descriptive answers may allow your partners to resolve situations for their current customers, thereby providing additional leads to you. The more detailed your presentation and answers to your partners' questions, the better the understanding they will have about what your business offers and who you can help. Take the time to get a better understanding of your partners' business and how they can help your clients. If you know how they can help individuals and why they take pride in their business, you will be better prepared to network with them. The greater understanding your referral partners have on how you can help their clients, the better chance you have on creating a long-term lead-generation partnership. When you receive a referral from your networking partners, make sure to provide excellent customer service and offer them the best options for their financial needs. Thank and keep your referral partners updated regarding the referral. Let them know you appreciate their partnership.

Referral relationships are a key component to long-term success as a loan officer. Maintaining referral relationships, staying in touch with your past customers, and growing your sphere of influence are the main factors to consistency. Your goal should be to create stability and maximize your income potential.

MEMBERSHIP AND GROUP PARTICIPATION

The following are a list of ideas to create, maintain, and expand relationships among your referral partners.

Whether you create or join a networking group, the following suggestions should be part of the group's bylaws.

1. The meetings should be held at least once per week at a convenient time and location for all members.
2. Membership and recruitment meetings should be held quarterly to attract additional members.
3. Set a minimum standard of time in business, and research potential new members through social-media sites and the Internet before they are considered for membership.
4. All members should complement each other's services. Only one member per occupation should be in the group. This will eliminate competition among members. All members in the networking group should be from a related profession. Every member should be responsible for enlisting new networking partners.

The more successful the group becomes with trading referrals and lead generation, the more valuable they will be to your success. Members should have a win-win attitude to maximize success for all.

The following list is the foundation for an effective networking group.

Many individuals may be helpful in your networking endeavors. Finding the right group of individuals to partner with and promote your business is the key to long-term success. A small number of like-minded interconnected people are far more valuable than a larger group of individuals. These individuals should have a good reputation in their occupations, be knowledgeable, and be experienced. Networking success should only be seen as win-win. Always take special care of your referrals; your reputation and future success will reply on the referrals' feedback to your networking partners.

Plan and track. Always plan any networking events you attend, and track how many leads you receive from each event you attend. Always ask for referrals in your area of expertise. Your networking partnerships rely on a thorough understanding of what you specialize in and what type of leads you are looking for.

Always keep an optimistic attitude; be pleasant, be positive, and smile. Your positive attitude can be contagious to your networking partners and help you create new relationships. Always be positive.

Long-term success in networking relationships is built upon a foundation of openness, friendliness, and a positive attitude.

As with all successful relationships, an effective balance between work and home is necessary. Having a healthy balance between business and social activities will help you control and limit stress. Having a well-rounded life is also helpful to your networking relationships. A well-balanced life will help your confidence and help you develop your skills to deal with all personality types you will encounter in your networking endeavors.

Having good life balance contributes directly to people believing in you. It enables you to clearly handle and resolve problems, show compassion, and demonstrate your integrity.

Long-term success in networking depends on developing a codependency with your lead referral partners. Creating a win-win relationship with your sphere of influence through sending and receiving quality and consistent referrals is the key to sustained success.

Attend public meetings to grow your sphere of influence. Look on your city's, county, and nonprofit agency's websites for meetings open to the public. These meetings may include but are not limited to real-estate boards, volunteer organizations, and planning and economic development agencies. Your local chamber of commerce is a great way to meet like-minded businesspeople. There are usually numerous events or meetings held each month. At these meetings, network and try to establish collaborative partnerships with individuals in complementary businesses. Loan officers are typically able to provide and receive leads from real-estate agents, insurance agents, accountants, attorneys, and contractors. Teaming up with individuals in these businesses will exponentially increase your marketing and reach to new customers. Be positive, reciprocate with leads, communicate effectively, and provide great customer service.

Chapter 8

ACCEPTING CHANGE AND THRIVING

The mortgage industry has been through an incredible amount of change over the past ten years. There have been countless government regulations and laws that have turned the mortgage business upside down. Keep in mind that the whole industry is affected by new regulations. It is important to accept change and challenge yourself to understand the nuances of the new guidelines as quickly as possible. This will give you an advantage over your competition. Keep an open dialogue with your compliance and underwriting departments so that you can manage the changes and decrease the time needed to understand and effectively implement the changes. Knowledge of future changes and open dialogue will help change to happen smoothly.

You may have to change the way you have been operating as a loan officer. Change is not easy, but acceptance and immediate knowledge of forthcoming changes will help you control your environment. Government regulations force changes to occur. Although new regulations and laws can pose challenges, if properly managed, they can make you even more competitive.

Determine what ideas you can implement in your daily routine and what changes will maximize your sales. Create a business plan to implement these ideas and changes. When you learn of new impending governmental regulations that will affect you as a mortgage professional, take the time to master and add these changes to your daily routine. Managing change will make processing and closing your business more efficient.

Keep your sphere of influence, business partners, potential new lead sources, and clients informed of upcoming changes to the mortgage industry. This will make you the go-to person for understanding how this will affect them and their business. The updates and information you provide to your associates and clients may be invaluable and make you an expert for the upcoming new requirements in mortgage banking. This may also allow you to distribute information and promote a new product.

CREATING A WINNING MARKETING PLAN

Proper implementation your new, improved marketing plan is essential. Study your options, review it carefully, and highlight any parts of your business plan that might be cumbersome. Prepare for any part of your marketing plan that might create issues, delays, or problems.

Create a list of goals, a step-by-step outline of tasks that need to be completed. Be sure to let anyone involved know what the final result should be and why it is important to thoroughly follow through with your plan. This includes your processor, underwriting, and real-estate partners.

STAYING CURRENT ON PRODUCT GUIDELINES AND REGULATORY CHANGES

When you work in an industry as regulated as mortgage banking, the only sure thing is change. The Dodd-Frank regulatory reform has brought constant change in the financial industry. Knowledge of new or updated regulations is a key component of managing the change and increasing your sales numbers and profitability.

The mortgage industry is an ever-changing, competitive environment. You have to keep up with the new regulations and trends; these changes will create opportunities to close more loans and grow your sphere of influence.

The earlier you detect opportunities, the greater the competitive edge you will have over your competition. Knowledge of upcoming changes will also create an advantage and show you are an expert in mortgage banking. When someone has a questions or problems, you will be the first one he or she calls to solve his or her issues.

The Internet is a great way to stay on top of relevant news and trends.

It is important to create time in your day to devote to changes and news regarding the mortgage industry. Schedule time daily or weekly reading about industry changes, new products, and networking. Staying up to date requires a regular commitment.

CONCLUSION

Find a Mentor: Establishing the mentor relationship creates firsthand knowledge of what it takes to become successful. Instantly applying these traits and activities to your business plan will eliminate sales by trial and error and increased the odds of success. Newly licensed loan officers assisting their mentors with daily sales functions will increase their knowledge of the mortgage profession and teach the necessary information to become successful. Guidance and advice from the mentor is an invaluable commodity.

Value of a Business Plan (create routine, set goals, outline weekly, monthly and annual plan, and determine desired income): A business plan is a plan of action created to ensure all avenues are being used for success. Many business plans start with the end goal. For instance, the goal may be $300,000 in sales revenue. When creating the business plan, individuals must carefully consider their strengths and weaknesses, time, and financial resources they have to achieve their goals. Set realistic goals. Building upon last year's sales and income, as well as understanding the current market situation, should play an important role in creating the business plan. An example of a business plan is as follows:

Income goal for the calendar year $
Sales needed
Floor time
Cold calls per week
Mailings per month
Prospects
Past customers
Farming area
Contract potential alternative lead sources
Mortgage companies, banks, and credit unions
Title companies
Interoffice referrals
Builders
Update active sellers and buyers weekly
Attend sales meetings, share ideas, listen to successful Realtors' advice
Attend educational and motivational seminars
Calculate the amount of time needed to devote to real estate per week
Daily hours needed to achieve goals
Deduct for days off
Deduct for vacations
Create a budget

Hard Work (building your business, taking risks): Determination, hard work, and perseverance are key to long-term success in the mortgage profession, but the profession may allow you to do more than most other occupations. Many loan professionals have a strong belief from their upbringing that hard work equals success. It is important to understand that sales is a numbers game; you have to follow a plan to reach so many potential clients to achieve your desired numbers.

People-Friendly Personality: You need to like people. If you do not like people, mortgage sales is not the career for you. Have the attitude that your clients' interests always come before yours. Your customers know if you are putting your interests before theirs.

Education (knowledge, ethics): The importance of education and in the mortgage industry allows you to stand out from other loan officers. Knowledge will make you an expert and the go-to person for specific loans in your market. This theme is interconnected to the value of a mentor.

Balance between Work and Family (time management, own your schedule, stress management, empowering yourself): Mortgage loan officers are typically commission-based; therefore, their time is money. Developing a system that efficiently uses time will not only increase income but will also relieve other pressures that accompany employment based on commission income. Effective time management will allow you to maximize your time and increase your accomplishments. Planning your day by creating a priority list of tasks that need to be completed will allow you to focus on activities that must be completed. Creating a list of other tasks that need to be completed by a certain date or that could be delegated will allow time to be focused on more important activities. Prioritizing your tasks will create focus will create proficiently. Balance is the key to having a long-term successful career. Maintaining a strong family life is more important than business. Many highly successful loan officers struggle with the concept of balance, and it is important to understand the value of balance before it negatively affects your life.

Advertising/Marketing (efficient use of resources, marketing strategy): Success as a commission-based loan officer requires a plan that uses your best characteristics and traits. Once you have decided how to market yourself based on your best qualities, developing a business plan and deciding how much you can financially devote to your business is your next step. When your business grows, you can increase your marketing budget accordingly. Your budget should include all your marketing activities, education, and other expenses, such as office assistants. The difference between success and failure may be as simple as following through on your plan. If your sales are less than expected or if you are busier than expected, pausing your investment in yourself and marketing efforts will only create ups and downs in your business. Ensuring a steady flow of business will require a continuous investment in yourself and your marketing plan. Commitment to a continuous marketing plan and personal investment is key to your business's success.

Think of cost-effective ways to advertise to save money. Some suggestions include creating your own flyers and brochures, researching alternative publications for advertising, dropping off flyers door to door instead of mailing, and using e-mail advertising as much as possible. Successful mortgage originators set aside 10 percent to 15 percent of their earnings to business expenses.

Building a Referral System (customer satisfaction, past customers, building a sphere of influence): Your past customers are the lifeblood of your business. It takes far more time and money to gain a new customer than to maintain a relationship with a past customer. Connecting with a past customer on a regular basis through phone calls, e-mails, and mailings is a great way to maintain a relationship. A follow-up call when his or her house transfers and a mailing just to say "thank you and congratulations on the purchase of your new home" will increase referrals from past clients and will let your customer know you will be around to help him or her after the transaction is completed. Building a file on each customer—such as birthdays, the anniversary date of the purchase of the house, the number of houses that he or she owns, and his or her occupation—may all be helpful in keeping communication open with your past customers. Maintaining a regular communication line with your past customers (for instance, once every four months), possibly calling them to see if they need your expertise or if a new program or a rate update for possible refinancing, is the foundation to a lead-generating system. Create a sense of loyalty with your past customers; it is the fastest and least expensive avenue to referral business.

There are a great number of factors that affect the success of mortgage loan officers. However, emphasizing the practices, traits, and characteristics of highly successful mortgage professionals will fabricate a fuller picture of how to achieve a high level of long-term success as a licensed mortgage loan officer. Hopefully, the descriptions, behaviors, and suggestions within this book will create an outline for long-term success in mortgage banking with a healthy balance between work and family time and obligations.

CPSIA information can be obtained
at www.ICGtesting.com
Printed in the USA
BVHW041820240621
610393BV00014B/457